CEC Mini-Library

**Exceptional
Children At Risk**

Hidden Youth:
Dropouts from
Special Education

Donald L. MacMillan

Published by The Council for Exceptional Children

A Product of the ERIC Clearinghouse
on Handicapped and Gifted Children

Library of Congress Catalog Card Number 91-58306

ISBN 0-86586-211-7

A product of the ERIC / OSEP Special Project, the ERIC Clearinghouse on Handicapped and Gifted Children

Published in 1991 by The Council for Exceptional Children, 1920 Association Drive, Reston, Virginia 22091-1589
Stock No. P354

Preparation of this book was supported in part by Grant #H023C80072 from the U.S. Office of Education.

This publication was prepared with funding from the U.S. Department of Education, Office of Special Education Programs, contract no. RI88062007. Contractors undertaking such projects under government sponsorship are encouraged to express freely their judgment in professional and technical matters. Prior to publication the manuscript was submitted for critical review and determination of professional competence. This publication has met such standards. Points of view, however, do not necessarily represent the official view or opinions of either The Council for Exceptional Children or the Department of Education.

Printed in the United States of America
10 9 8 7 6 5 4 3 2 1

Contents

Each book in the series pertains to one of the conference strands. Each provides a synthesis of the literature in its area, followed by practical suggestions—derived from the literature—for program developers, administrators, and teachers. The 11 books in the series are as follows:

- *Programming for Aggressive and Violent Students* addresses issues that educators and other professionals face in contending with episodes of violence and aggression in the schools.

- *Abuse and Neglect of Exceptional Children* examines the role of the special educator in dealing with children who are abused and neglected and those with suspected abuse and neglect.

- *Special Health Care in the School* provides a broad-based definition of the population of students with special health needs and discusses their unique educational needs.

- *Homeless and in Need of Special Education* examines the plight of the fastest growing segment of the homeless population, families with children.

- *Hidden Youth: Dropouts from Special Education* addresses the difficulties of comparing and drawing meaning from dropout data prepared by different agencies and examines the characteristics of students and schools that place students at risk for leaving school prematurely.

- *Born Substance Exposed, Educationally Vulnerable* examines what is known about the long-term effects of exposure *in utero* to alcohol and other drugs, as well as the educational implications of those effects.

- *Depression and Suicide: Special Education Students at Risk* reviews the role of school personnel in detecting signs of depression and potential suicide and in taking appropriate action, as well as the role of the school in developing and implementing treatment programs for this population.

- *Language Minority Students with Disabilities* discusses the preparation needed by schools and school personnel to meet the needs of limited-English-proficient students with disabilities.

- *Alcohol and Other Drugs: Use, Abuse, and Disabilities* addresses the issues involved in working with children and adolescents who have disabling conditions and use alcohol and other drugs.

- *Rural, Exceptional, At Risk* examines the unique difficulties of delivering education services to at-risk children and youth with exceptionalities who live in rural areas.

Foreword

EXCEPTIONAL CHILDREN AT RISK
CEC Mini-Library

Many of today's pressing social problems, such as poverty, homelessness, drug abuse, and child abuse, are factors that place children and youth at risk in a variety of ways. There is a growing need for special educators to understand the risk factors that students must face and, in particular, the risks confronting children and youth who have been identified as exceptional. A child may be at risk *due to* a number of quite different phenomena, such as poverty or abuse. Therefore, the child may be at risk *for* a variety of problems, such as developmental delays; debilitating physical illnesses or psychological disorders; failing or dropping out of school; being incarcerated; or generally having an unrewarding, unproductive adulthood. Compounding the difficulties that both the child and the educator face in dealing with these risk factors is the unhappy truth that a child may have more than one risk factor, thereby multiplying his or her risk and need.

The struggle within special education to address these issues was the genesis of the 1991 CEC conference "Children on the Edge." The content for the conference strands is represented by this series of publications, which were developed through the assistance of the Division of Innovation and Development of the U.S. Office of Special Education Programs (OSEP). OSEP funds the ERIC/OSEP Special Project, a research dissemination activity of The Council for Exceptional Children. As a part of its publication program, which synthesizes and translates research in special education for a variety of audiences, the ERIC/OSEP Special Project coordinated the development of this series of books and assisted in their dissemination to special education practitioners.

- *Double Jeopardy: Pregnant and Parenting Youth in Special Education* addresses the plight of pregnant teenagers and teenage parents, especially those in special education, and the role of program developers and practitioners in responding to their educational needs.

Background information applicable to the conference strand on juvenile corrections can be found in another publication, *Special Education in Juvenile Corrections*, which is a part of the CEC Mini-Library *Working with Behavioral Disorders*. That publication addresses the demographics of incarcerated youth and promising practices in responding to their needs.

1. Introduction

Dropout rates are being used by some as educational indicators of quality and to gauge the holding power of special education programs. Different agencies use different accounting procedures for estimating graduation and dropout rates.

Policy makers use dropout rates as key indicators of success for educational programs at the federal and state levels. Public Law 100-297, the Hawkins-Stafford Elementary and Secondary School Improvement Amendments of 1988, requires the Commissioner of the National Center for Education Statistics (NCES) to report annually the number and rate of dropouts nationwide. Interest in this outcome extends to special education, as evidenced by the provisions of Section 618 (b)(3) of the Education of the Handicapped Act amendments of 1983 (P. L. 98-199) and 1986 (P. L.99-457), which direct the Secretary of Education to obtain data on children and youth with disabilities who are exiting the educational system and to report findings by disability category and age. These data have been reported by the Office of Special Education Programs (OSEP) beginning with the 1984–1985 school year and continuing to the present. Dropout data are considered by some to indicate the so-called "holding power" of special education programs. That is, the lower the dropout rate reported, the greater the appeal of the program. At another level, however, the intent of Public Law 94-142, the Education for All Handicapped Children Act of 1975, was to serve students until graduation or age 21.

Evidence that students with disabilities are not availing themselves of these services is reason for concern. Research examining dropout rates of students with disabilities (e.g., Edgar, 1987; Jay & Padilla, 1987; Zigmond & Thornton, 1985) suggests that the rate of dropping out is higher for certain categories of students with disabilities than for the general population. Studies that directly compare the rates for students with and without disabilities have been conducted only on a small-scale basis. One problem with research of this type is that there is a need to standardize definitions of dropouts and accounting procedures across agencies and studies (MacMillan, Balow, Widaman, Borthwick-Duffy, & Hendrick, 1990). A discussion of this problem, as well as comparison of the OSEP exiting data with those of other agencies such as the National Center for Education Statistics and the U.S. Census Bureau, is provided in this book.

Being able to predict which students are at risk for dropping out is fundamental to any effort to prevent them from dropping out. Efforts to date suggest that certain child characteristics, school history factors, and family factors (Wolman, Bruininks, & Thurlow, 1989) are predictive of leaving school early; the next step is to design effective prevention programs and to evaluate their effectiveness. Researchers and practitioners have undertaken preliminary efforts in this direction. This book presents the evidence on their effectiveness.

2. Synthesis of Research

Despite the difficulty in comparing data from different agencies, evidence suggests higher dropout rates for children with mild disabilities, particularly for students with learning disabilities and with emotional disturbance.

Research on school dropouts among special education populations can be organized into studies or reports that (a) establish the magnitude of the problem, (b) identify predictors or correlates of those at risk for dropping out, and (c) evaluate the effectiveness of programs to reduce the numbers of dropouts. The first two endeavors have attracted much more attention in the research literature than the last.

Magnitude of the Dropout Problem

OSEP has reported annually on the exiting behavior of special education students by age and disability category for every year since 1984–1985 in the *Annual Reports* (OSEP, 1987a, 1988, 1989, 1990). Exiting students are tabulated by age and disability and according to the route by which they left the educational system (graduation with diploma, graduation with certificate, reached maximum age, dropped out, and status unknown). It is important to note that *OSEP requests that only students who formally withdrew from school without completing their educational program be counted as dropouts.* In other words, a student who simply stops attending but fails to formally withdraw is not to be counted as a dropout but will be counted in the "status unknown" category. Table 1 shows the national summary for the *Twelfth Annual Report* (OSEP, 1990). Figures reported here reflect the number and percentage of students who exited the educational system (not the total number served) according to the avenue by which they exited. The table shows that 27.40% of all special education students who exited the educational system did so by dropping out of school. As discussed later, the data reported by OSEP do not reflect dropout or graduation rates for a known grade or age cohort; therefore, it cannot be inferred that the reciprocal of the dropout figure reported by OSEP is the graduation rate.

TABLE 1

**Number and Percentage of Students with Disabilities
14 Years of Age or Older Exiting the Educational System:
National Summary for 1988–1989**

	Graduation Diploma	Graduation Certificate	Maximum Age	Dropout	Status Unknown
Number	100,075	26,830	5,957	65,310	40,161
Percentage[a]	41.99	11.26	2.50	27.40	16.85

[a] Denominator for computing the percentage is the total exiting the educational system; not the total number of special education students served who are 14 years of age or older.

Source: Office of Special Education Programs, U.S. Department of Education. (1990). *Twelfth Annual Report to Congress on the Implementation of the Education of the Handicapped Act.* Washington, DC: Author.

The summary figures obscure the fact that tremendous variation exists among states in the cases falling under each of the categories. For example, the report of the OSEP Task Force for the Improvement of Data on School Exit Status (Westat, 1991) gives the minimum and maximum value under each of the exit bases, which is shown in Table 2. It is evident that some states report virtually no students dropping out or exiting via the "other/unknown" category, whereas others report nearly half of their special education exiters leaving through these routes. The median values shown in the third column of figures provide one estimate of the average value reported by states for each of these exiting routes.

Some states do not award certificates of attendance or alternative diplomas, but give a diploma to everyone who completes a high school

TABLE 2

**Range of State Percentages of Students with Disabilities Exiting the
Educational System by Basis of Exit: 1988–1989**

Basis of Exit	Minimum	Maximum	Median
Graduation with diploma	12.13	87.18	44.00
Graduation with certificate	0.00	57.75	9.70
Reached maximum age	0.28	6.54	2.23
Dropped out	0.81	48.18	26.71
Other/unknown	0.00	56.87	17.36

Source: Westat. (October, 1990). *Counting secondary school completers: Threats to the comparability of the OSEP exiting data* (p. 10). Washington, DC: Office of Special Education Programs, U.S. Department of Education.

program of study. Others make extensive use of the certificate as an exiting document (note in Table 2 the range from 0 to 57.75% of exiters receiving certificates in various states). Such variations in policy and accounting procedures greatly confuse any attempt to estimate the magnitude of the dropout problem among special education students.

Overall dropout estimates for the general school population have not increased dramatically in recent years. High school completion rates are reported by several federal agencies. Table 3 shows the percentages completing high school for the years 1970–1989 as reported by the Bureau of the Census, the National Center for Education Statistics (NCES), and the Department of Education. All three databases yield completion rates between 70% and 77%, although they arrive at these numbers very differently (see Frase, 1989). In fact, according to Frase the graduation/completion rate increased every decade from 1869–1870 until the 1970s. In the late 1960s, the completion rate did not increase, and during the 1970s it actually decreased by about 5%, a trend that reversed somewhat in the 1980s (Frase, 1989, p. 72).

Some analysts interpret the complement of these figures (i.e., 100% minus the percentage completing) as the dropout rate; that would make the national dropout rate approximately 25%. The error in making such an interpretation, as discussed by Frase (1989), Kominski (1990), and MacMillan and colleagues (1990), is that some students continue to work toward graduation even though they have not completed on time.

To estimate dropout rates, decision rules must be established regarding (a) the definition of a dropout, (b) how rates will be computed (e.g., for 1 year, 4 years), (c) the cohort to be followed, and (d) exclusions that should not be counted in estimating the rate (e.g., deaths, students retained in grade). Table 4 summarizes these considerations as they pertain to the federal agencies that monitor school completion and dropout rates. The U.S. Census Bureau and NCES both use the Current Population Survey data that reflect the percentage of individuals of a given age (e.g., 16–17 years) who report that they have graduated from high school (MacMillan et al., in press.) The U.S. Department of Education, however, uses data supplied by states and compares the number of graduates to those students who were enrolled as ninth graders 4 years earlier, regardless of their age. In contrast, the OSEP database uses neither an age cohort nor a grade cohort. Instead, it considers only the total number of students receiving special education services who exited the school system during the school year. Since OSEP combines age cohorts and grade cohorts, its estimates cannot be compared to percentages reported by the other agencies.

OSEP is the only agency to report separately on students with disabilities and on the various routes by which such students exit the educational system—diploma, certificate, maximum age, dropout, and unknown. However, recent analyses of the OSEP accounting proce-

TABLE 3
Alternative Measures Related to Completing
High School: 1970–1989

Year	Percentage of 18–19 Year Olds		High School Graduates as Percentage of 17 Year Olds[b] (School Year Ending)	Graduates as Percentage of Ninth Graders 4 Years Before[c] (School Year Ending)
	Completed High School[a] or Enrolled Below College	Completed High School[a]		
	(October)			
	(1)	(2)	(3)	(4)
1970	83.8	73.3	76.9	—
1971	84.7	73.2	75.9	—
1972	85.3	74.9	75.5	—
1973	84.0	74.0	75.5	—
1974	83.4	73.4	74.4	—
1975	84.0	73.7	73.6	—
1976	83.4	73.1	73.7	—
1977	83.4	72.9	73.9	—
1978	83.3	73.5	73.0	—
1979	83.2	72.8	72.0	—
1980	84.3	73.7	71.4	—
1981	84.0	72.5	71.8	—
1982	83.3	72.0	72.7	69.5
1983	85.5	72.7	73.3	—
1984	84.8	73.3	73.7	70.8
1985	85.7	74.6	73.2	71.7
1986	87.9[d,e]	74.6[d,e]	73.0	71.6
1987	86.7[e]	73.6[e]	73.0	71.1
1988	85.4[e]	71.5[e]	73.9[f]	—
1989	—	—	74.0[f]	—

— Not available.

[a] Includes graduates of public and private high schools and recipients of equivalency credentials.

[b] Includes graduates of regular day school programs in private and public high schools. Does not include recipients of equivalency credentials.

[c] Public schools only; does not include recipients of equivalency credentials. Adjusted for state migration rates and unclassified students.

[d] Data revised from previously published.

[e] Data based on different editing procedures than in earlier years.

[f] Estimated.

Sources: U.S. Department of Commerce, Bureau of the Census, "School Enrollment—Social and Economic Characteristics of Students, October" (various years), *Current Population Reports*, Series P-20, and unpublished tabulations; U.S. Department of Education, National Center for Education Statistics, *Digest of Education Statistics, 1989*, forthcoming; and U.S. Department of Education, Office of Planning, Budget and Evaluation, State Education Statistics (Secretary's Wall Chart), various years.

TABLE 4
**Comparison of Different Agencies' Approaches to
Estimating Dropout Rates**

Agency	Type of Rate Measured	Cohort	Denominator	Exemptions
U.S. Census Bureau	STATUS	Age (e.g., 16–17 yr.)	Total population in age range.	Delayed completers— i.e., those still enrolled. Recipients of equivalent high school certificate.
NCES	STATUS[a]	Age	Number of students in CPS sample in age range.	Delayed completers.
	COHORT[b]	1980 sophomore class	Total number in sophomore class in 1980.	
U.S. Department of Education "Wall Chart"	COHORT		Number of students in ninth grade 4 years earlier.	Adjusts ninth grade enrollments for students unclassified by grade. None—must have received regular high school diploma to be counted as a high school completer.
OSEP	EVENT	Academic year	Total number special education students exiting the educational system.	None—attempts to account for all special education students exiting the educational system on the basis for exiting.

Note: NCES = National Center for Education Statistics; OSEP = Office of Special Education Programs.

[a] NCES used the Current Population Survey (CPS) data from the annual October household survey.
[b] NCES supplements the CPS data with data from the *High School and Beyond* data, which followed a grade cohort; i.e., the sophomore class of 1980.

From "Special Education Students Exiting the Educational System" by D. L. MacMillan, K. F. Widaman, I. H. Balow, S. Borthwick-Duffy, R. E. Hemsley, & I. G. Hendrick, in press, *The Journal of Special Education.* Copyright 1991 by PRO-ED, Inc. Reprinted by permission.

dures (Westat, 1990, 1991) have raised serious questions regarding the way different states use the "unknown" category. Some states use it to count students who have left *special education* but remain in school (e.g., a child with an articulation disorder who is no longer receiving speech therapy). Although the OSEP data cannot be compared directly to data reported by other agencies, they do provide a picture of the students with disabilities who are exiting the educational system that is neither better nor worse than the picture provided by the other agencies. It is fair to say, however, that the OSEP data do not reveal what percentage of a given category of children with disabilities drop out of school for a given age or grade cohort.

Some smaller scale projects do permit comparisons of dropout rates of children with and without disabilities. Edgar (1987), Wolman and colleagues (1989), and Zigmond and Thornton (1985) have provided more detailed reviews of this research. In fact, the general finding that the percentage of certain categories of students with disabilities among dropouts is considerably higher than that reported for students without disabilities has been reason for concern. Evidence suggests that the rate of dropping out is higher for certain special education categories (e.g., learning disabled [LD] and emotionally disturbed [ED]); however, the lack of comparable definitions and accounting systems and the cohort differences preclude definitive conclusions regarding this point.

Dropout rates for students with disabilities vary as a function of disability category and certain program features. For example, the dropout rates reported for students categorized as having emotional disturbance and learning disabilities are higher than those reported for other disability categories (OSEP, 1987a, 1988, 1989, 1990; Wolman et al., 1989). In other research, Edgar (1987) reported that 42% of students categorized as LD and ED dropped out, whereas only 18% of students with mental retardation, 12% of those with severe disabilities, and 8% of those with sensory disabilities left school early.

There are several plausible explanations for the differential between students with mild and severe disabilities. For example, learners with mild disabilities who are employable outside school and enjoy little success in school may have the option of leaving school early to go to work. Students with more severe disabilities, on the other hand, may have less freedom of choice and lack the option of leaving school. Another possibility is that students with mild disabilities may prefer leaving school to having to compete in mainstreamed classes, which is where they are often assigned. Further research is needed to explain this differential. Table 5 summarizes studies on dropouts among students with disabilities (Wolman et al. 1989).

TABLE 5
Characteristics of Studies That Have Investigated Dropouts in Special Education

Study	Population	SES	Methods to calculate dropout rates	Community type	Dropout criteria	Dropout rate	Employment rate
Bernoff (1981)	Students from SpEd schools	All social classes	1-year cross-sectional (1979-80)	Urban	Dropped from school's rolls for specific cause or because whereabouts of student unknown	Special schools, 2% General schools, 5.4%	—
Bruck (1985)	Persons with LD	Middle classes	Dropout percentage across different class years	—	—	10%	—
Bruininks et al. (1988)	Persons with LD, SP, MR, & ED	White, middle class	Dropout percentage across 8 class yrs.	Suburban community	Leaving school without graduating; moving students or GED students were not considered dropouts	SpEd group, 28%; Two control groups (without handicaps), 2% & 5%. Subjects with special impairment, 12%; with MR, 19%; with LD, 28%; & with ED, 73%	—
Cobb & Crump (1984)	Persons with LD	Mostly lower-middle class or upper-lower class	Dropout percentage across several class yrs.	Nonurban, mostly agricultural county	Student who was dropped from rolls of school system & who did not reenter another school system	42%	—

TABLE 5 (Continued)

Study	Population	SES	Methods to calculate dropout rates	Community type	Dropout criteria	Dropout rate	Employment rate
Edgar (1987)	Persons with LD & ED; subjects with MR, SH, & SI	—	1-year cross-sectional (1984-85)	Urban	Leaving school system before graduation. Age-outs were not considered dropouts	Total: 35%, 42% with LD; 18% with MR; 12% with SH; 8% with SI	Dropouts = 28%; graduates & age-outs = 48%
Fafard & Haubrich (1981)	Persons with LD	White middle class	Dropout percentage across 8 class yrs.	Suburban community	—	14%	—
Fardig et al. (1985)	Persons with mild handicaps (73% with MR)	—	Percentage completing 12th grade across several class yrs.	Rural	Not finishing 12th grade	31%	—
Hasazi et al. (1985)	64% of subjects in resource rooms (students with mild handicaps)	—	Dropout percentage across 5 class yrs.	Rural, urban, and metropolitan districts	Exit from school prior to age 18 without graduating; 18 yrs or older who left school not considered dropouts.	28% dropped from school; 13% left school at 18 or older without graduating	51% dropout; 30% left school at 18 or over; 60% graduated.
Hess & Lauber (1985)	Students in SpEd schools	All social classes	Cohort study	Urban	Leaving school before graduation	Special schools, 65.3%; general schools, 43%	—

9

TABLE 5 (Continued)

Study	Population	SES	Methods to calculate dropout rates	Community type	Dropout criteria	Dropout rate	Employment rate
Hewitt (1981)	Persons with LD	White, middle class	No dropout rate calculated	Suburban	—	—	Dropouts with LD, 44%; Graduates with LD, 58%
Hoffman et al. (1987)	Persons with LD	Mostly white	Percentage of graduates across different class yrs. & different states	—	Data reported about students who did not receive HS diploma or GED	37%	—
Levin, E., et al. (1985)	Persons with LD	—	Cohort study (students in 9th grade in 1977-78 were followed 4 yrs later)	Urban	Stopped attending school; GED or alternative certificate students were considered dropouts	51%	—
Lichtenstein (1987)	Students self-identified as having handicaps	Highly stratified national sample including all SES	Cohort study (4-yr period)	Stratified national sample including all community types	Leaving HS before graduation	Students who self-identified as having LD, 37%; as having HI, 28%; as having SP, 24%	Dropouts with handicaps often employed full-time unemployed, or not in labor force

TABLE 5 (Continued)

Study	Population	SES	Methods to calculate dropout rates	Community type	Dropout criteria	Dropout rate	Employment rate
New York City Board of Education (1985)	Students in SpEd schools	All social classes	1-yr cross-sectional, & 4-yr estimation	Urban	Students who left school. GED not considered dropouts. "Not found" students considered dropouts	Special schools, 23% (66%, 4-yr estimation) general schools, 13%; 42%, 4-yr estimation	—
Owings & Stocking (1986)	Students self-identified as having handicaps	Highly stratified national sample including all SES	Cohort study (1-yr period, 1980-1982)	Stratified national sample including all community types	Leaving HS before graduation	Students who self-identified as having handicaps, 19.1%; control group, 12.6%	—
Porter (1982)	Students with handicaps	—	—	—	Students who dropped out of school without earning a HS diploma	—	Dropouts, 70%; graduates, 87.5%
Stephenson (1985)	Exceptional students	All ethnic groups & immigrant students in Miami, FL	Cohort study (4.5 yr period)	—	Students who left the K-12 program before completion and receiving a certificate or diploma	Exceptional students, 40%; general, 30%	—

TABLE 5 (Continued)

Study	Population	SES	Methods to calculate dropout rates	Community type	Dropout criteria	Dropout rate	Employment rate
U.S. Department of Education (1987) (Census data)	All levels of handicaps & all categories	All social classes	1-yr cross-sectional (1984-85 school yr)	All community types	Students actually known to have dropped out. Students who simply stopped coming to school or whose status was unknown not included	Total, 21%; students with LD, 19%; ED, 29%; MR, 23%; SP, 17%; HI, 12%; multi-other, 13%; handicaps, 20%; OI, 11%; VI, 14%; deaf-blind, 16%	—
U.S. Department of Education (1988) (Census data)	All levels of handicaps & all categories	All social classes	1-yr cross-sectional (1985-86 school yr)	All community types	Students who were actually known to have dropped out; students who simply stopped coming to school or whose status was unknown not included	Total, 26%; students with LD, 47%; students with MR, 23%; students with ED, 21%	—
White et al. (1980)	Persons with LD	Middle class	Percentage of HS diplomas across several school yrs	Suburb of a metro area	No definition of dropout. Data reported about percentage of students who received HS diploma, occupational certificate, or GED	26% did not earn a HS diploma; 2.2% did not receive any degree (GED or occupational certificate)	—

TABLE 5 (Continued)

Study	Population	SES	Methods to calculate dropout rates	Community type	Dropout criteria	Dropout rate	Employment rate
Zigmond & Thornton (1985)	Persons with LD	—	Cohort study (students in 9th grade in 1978-79 were followed 6 yrs later)	Urban	Stopped attending school	Control group, 54.2%; students wtih LD, 32.8%	Dropouts with LD, 43.8%; nondropouts with LD, 74.1%

Note. SpEd = special education; LD = learning disabilities; SP = speech impairment; MR = mental retardation; ED = emotional disturbance; BD = behavioral disturbance; SH = severe handicaps; SI = sensory impairment; HS = high school; GED = General Educational Development certificate; SES = socioeconomic status; HI = hearing impairment; OI = orthopedic impairment; VI = visual impairment.

From "Dropouts and Dropout Programs: Implications for Special Education" by C. Wolman, R. Bruininks, & M. L. Thurlow, 1989, *Remedial and Special Education 10*(5), pp. 6–20, 50. Copyright 1989 by PRO-ED, Inc. Reprinted by permission.

Predicting Who Will Drop Out of School

The research literature contains numerous reports of factors that are predictive of, or place the student at higher risk for, dropping out of school before completion. Most research concerning prediction has been concentrated in regular education, and the question of whether or not the predictors for the general population hold true for children with disabilities requires further study. This section summarizes these factors under various headings. The following sources were consulted in creating these summary lists: Barro and Kolstad (1987), Ekstrom, Goertz, Pollack, and Rock (1986), Fine (1986), Frase (1989), Peng and Takai (1983), Rumberger (1987), Rumberger, Ghatak, Poulos, Ritter, and Dornbusch (1990), and Wolman and colleagues (1989).

It is important to distinguish between *predictors* of dropping out and *reasons for*, or *causes of*, dropping out. To illustrate, a greater risk exists for certain ethnic minority group children to drop out; yet if one were to question the student, he or she would not say that the reason for or cause of dropping out was ethnic group membership. Research has most often consisted of retrospective studies of a class of students (e.g., those projected to graduate in June 1989). That is, the investigator begins by creating lists of those who graduated and those who did not and then goes back into school records to identify evidence or data that might permit the prediction of these two outcomes. The investigator then examines student characteristics (e.g., gender, ethnic group) and school records (e.g., school history, attendance) in an attempt to identify factors that differentiate graduates from dropouts.

The following four factors have been found to predict dropping out among students without disabilities: individual/family characteristics, location, student behaviors, and school characteristics and experiences.

Individual/Family Characteristics. Several individual and family demographic and socioeconomic characteristics have emerged as predictive of higher dropout rates.

- Dropout rates for males are slightly higher than rates for females.

- Higher rates have been noted for African-Americans and Hispanics compared to Whites; however, the majority of dropouts are White because the majority of high school students are White.

- Dropout rates for American Indians/Alaskan Natives are relatively high, whereas rates for Asian students are relatively low.

- Dropout rates are higher for students coming from low socio-economic backgrounds, single-parent families, and from non-English-speaking family backgrounds.

- Higher dropout rates have been found for students coming from homes with weak educational or motivational support and from homes characterized by permissive parenting styles.

Location. The major location variable linked to higher dropout rates concerns inner-city as contrasted to suburban and other non-metropolitan locations.

- Central cities have higher dropout rates than are found in suburban or nonmetropolitan areas.
- African-Americans and Whites living in suburbs do not differ in dropout rates, nor do those living in urban centers.
- Dropout rates are higher in the South and West than in the Northeast.
- In the West, the dropout rate for Hispanic students is extremely high.

Student Behaviors. Among behaviors predictive of higher dropout rates are the following:

- Students who marry or have children before the time they would graduate show higher dropout rates.
- Students with a history of behavior problems with school authorities or the law are at greater risk for dropping out.
- Students reporting the use of drugs or other substances are more frequently dropouts than are students abstaining from using substances.
- Some evidence links having a job with higher dropout rates, but the number of hours worked appears to be more important than working per se.

School Characteristics and Experiences. Certain characteristics of schools have been related to dropout rates. In addition, a student's degree of success in school has been linked repeatedly to decisions to drop out.

- Higher dropout rates are found in schools that are overcrowded and that have an underachieving student body, high level of feeling of disempowerment among staff, tracking, weak leadership by the principal, and a low degree of order and discipline.
- Students with poor grades, who have repeated a grade, or who are overage for their grade are at at risk for dropping out.

- A history of school attendance problems, particularly large numbers of missed days for reasons other than illness, is predictive of dropping out.

Note that low achievement of students is used by some researchers to characterize the individual dropouts, whereas other researchers have used achievement to characterize *schools* in which there are high dropout rates. McDill, Natriello, and Pallas (1985) focused attention on the possibility that educational reform, particularly as it involves instituting higher academic standards, may increase dropout rates among that segment of the school population already at risk by virtue of other factors.

Predicting Dropouts Among Students with Disabilities

Relatively little research has examined whether or not the predictors of school dropout for the general school population are also predictive for students in special education in general and for specific categories in particular. Lichtenstein (1987) found that both general education and special education dropouts came from the lowest socioeconomic quartile, and dropouts from both groups were more often found in vocational (as opposed to academic) courses and were found to score in the lower quartiles on measures of cognitive ability. Zigmond and Thornton (1985) found more grade repetitions among dropouts (both with and without learning disabilities), with 90% of the students with learning disabilities who repeated a grade dropping out and 100% of the nondisabled students who repeated a grade dropping out. In addition, poor attendance and negative attitudes toward school have been found to characterize special education dropouts (Hewitt, 1981; Levin, E., Zigmond, & Birch, 1985).

Finally, preliminary findings from the National Longitudinal Transition Study (Lou Danielson, personal communication, November 28, 1990) suggest a higher dropout rate among students with disabilities who are mainstreamed as compared to their counterparts who are enrolled in more restrictive programs. Of course, this finding needs careful examination because students who are not amenable to mainstreaming may also have fewer employment opportunities to induce them to leave school, as mentioned earlier. In other words, the finding may reflect differences in student aptitudes or other characteristics rather than inadequacies inherent in mainstreaming.

OSEP has recently funded investigators in California, Minnesota, and Washington State to develop and validate intervention programs aimed at the junior high level. Findings from these projects should be forthcoming in the next few years and should help direct efforts at preventing school dropout.

3. Practitioner Implications

Teachers and administrators should be familiar with characteristics of students—and of schools—that place students at risk for early school leaving; and educators must be sensitive to the need for evaluation data on dropout prevention programs.

The knowledge base regarding dropouts is somewhat limited at this time; research has yet to address prevention in any sophisticated fashion. As noted previously, getting a handle on reliable and valid estimates of the magnitude of the dropout problem continues to be problematic. Until we know how many students, both with and without disabilities, are actually leaving school before graduation, it is difficult to address questions concerning prevention. Nevertheless, the issue of dropouts is high on the agenda of policymakers, and questions are frequently raised concerning how to prevent students from leaving school before graduation. What can be done at classroom, school, and district levels to reduce dropouts? At present, it is speculative to extrapolate from predictors (i.e., correlates) of dropping out to presumed reasons why students drop out. Moreover, many of the identified predictors such as low achievement and ethnic group membership are difficult, if not impossible, to modify.

The following sections present suggestions intended to minimize the likelihood of students' dropping out; however, these are offered only tentatively. Prevention measures must await refinement of dropout rate measures and identification of reasons precipitating dropout decisions. Such decisions are personal ones, and they are likely to be multiple and complex. Dropout prevention programs as they are currently structured frequently lack validation data and the consumer should beware.

Suggestions for Teachers

Teachers must be alert to those students in class who are at risk for dropping out of school.

The review of research in the previous section highlighted some of the predictors of dropping out, which can serve teachers in identifying students who are most at risk for dropping out. At the same time, teachers should be sensitive to the fact that these predictors merely indicate that these students are at risk; they should not be interpreted to suggest that all students exhibiting these characteristics will drop out. For example, students who are members of certain minority groups appear to be more likely to drop out of high school than are students from other ethnic groups. Therefore, a teacher might be more attuned to other predictors such as absence rate and low achievement that, if present in combination, place a particular minority group student highly at risk.

Teachers should also be aware that the predictors can serve as criteria against which student reviews can be performed. That is, when teachers and counselors periodically review student records, it might be helpful to do so with particular attention to those factors that appear to predict dropouts: consideration of a student's attendance; whether he or she is overage for grade; whether a grade has been repeated; any indication that the student has a history of substance abuse; school history concerning behavior problems; and, if known, the demographics of the home (language spoken, support for education, etc.). By performing such a review, the teacher can identify the extent to which a particular student might fit the profile of a likely dropout.

Teachers should be aware that the probability of high dropout rates is greater when certain school features are considered.

Inner-city schools appear to have a much greater problem with dropouts than do suburban or nonmetropolitan schools. Therefore, teachers and counselors working in inner-city schools should be more alert to the possibility that their students will leave school before graduation. In these schools, more staff time should be devoted to alerting teachers and counselors to the child and family factors that constitute a risk case. At back-to-school night, open house, or whenever teachers have access to parents in schools with high dropout rates, time should be devoted to explaining the costs of dropping out. Efforts can be made to engage parents and the community in prevention programs to minimize the dropout rate in those schools where it is occurring at high rates.

Teachers working with certain populations of special education students should be aware that the potential for dropping out is greater for these students than it is for others.

As the review of literature suggested, certain special education populations are particularly at risk for dropping out of school. The evidence to date suggests that students with learning disabilities and emotional disturbance are particularly prone to dropping out.

One possible suggestion to teachers of these two groups of students is to include in the curriculum serious discussion of the plight of dropouts. The literature is replete with evidence that high school dropouts are less successful in getting jobs and more inclined to get laid off when economic times are poor, and that even when they do secure a job, they tend to get jobs that pay less than those secured by high school graduates (see Catterall, 1988/1989).

Teachers and counselors must be sensitive to the gradual disengagement of students from school, intervene early, and work to counter feelings of isolation and alienation.

For a substantial number of dropouts, the decision to leave school is not made impulsively. Rather, a gradual disengagement can be seen, with attendance problems beginning in elementary school, increasing during middle school or junior high, and becoming chronic during high school. It is not enough to initiate dropout prevention programs in the 10th grade. Many students have already disengaged from school by this time, and even if they continue to attend physically on selected days, they have dropped out psychologically before their physical withdrawal. Comprehensive prevention efforts must involve teachers at the elementary, junior high, and high school levels to identify symptoms of disengagement and to target those students who evidence some of these symptoms.

In addition, self-reports of high school dropouts are reminiscent of findings in the Carnegie Report entitled *Turning Points* (Carnegie, 1989), which described many young adolescents as experiencing alienation. That is to say, many students do not believe that anyone at school really cares about them. Self-reports of dropouts suggest that no one sincerely tried to dissuade them from leaving school. Some students who leave school early might have remained if a teacher, counselor, coach, or principal had been sensitive to the fact that they were alienated from peers and needed more attention from or greater display of interest on the part of adults in their school careers. As the sign above the Orthogenic School at the University of Chicago reads, "Those children who are most difficult to love need love the most." It is easy for most teachers and classmates to relate positively to attractive, well-behaved, high-achieving students who are school leaders. However, the unattractive student who struggles academically and is inactive in school affairs is less likely to get spontaneous attention. Teachers and fellow students may need to make a concerted effort to take an interest in such a student's school affairs.

Teachers must recognize that there are many types of dropouts, and not attend only to the stereotype of the "typical" dropout.

The organization and presentation of research findings tend to promote the image of a typical dropout. Such a student attends an inner-city school, belongs to an ethnic minority group, struggles academically, and so on. In reality, there are as many reasons for dropping out as there are dropouts. Students who share the same personal academic characteristics or situations often reach very different decisions about continuing in school For example, although some pregnant teenagers drop out, others stay in school. A closer examination of an individual case is likely to reveal that the young woman who drops out, in addition to being pregnant, has other circumstances that contribute to the decision to leave school early. For example, she is also unsuccessful academically, has no aspirations to attend college, lives in a family that does not encourage academic achievement, and socializes with friends who do not attend school. Another pregnant teenager who does aspire to college, is successful in school, and socializes with friends who also plan to go to college might make a very different decision. Pregnancy may contribute to the decision to drop out, but it is only one of many factors that enter into it.

Furthermore, not *all* dropouts are having trouble academically. There are times and circumstances when the decision to leave school early is both reasonable and probably beneficial to the student. In such cases, the teacher should know when not to recommend staying in high school as the best alternative. Increasingly, students with excellent academic records are dropping out for various reasons. For example, high school campuses in certain areas are becoming physically dangerous with the increase in drug activity and gangs (see Handler, 1988/1989). After leaving high school, a student with a good academic record may immediately enroll at the community college and complete his or her education in a less threatening atmosphere. Other strong students leave school because of the necessity to assist their families financially. Teachers must open lines of communication so that students may share their reasons for making decisions, and teachers should critically evaluate the reasons these students give. Teachers must also be aware of alternative paths for students to accomplish the goal of graduating when circumstances at the high school are, in the student's opinion, not worth enduring.

Teachers should take an active role in policy-making at the school and district level, particularly as it affects standards for promotion and graduation. Unrealistic standards can contribute to the dropout problem.

The recent Westat (1991) report summarized a survey conducted by the National Association of State Directors of Special Education (NASDSE) to which all 50 states and the District of Columbia responded. States with minimum-competency-test requirements for graduation had lower percentages of students graduating with a diploma than did states without such requirements (39.7% compared to 47.1%); and states with minimum competency tests graduated a lower percentage of special education students (70.6%) than did states without this requirement (75.1%).

The research cited in the previous section by McDill and colleagues (1985) implicated the recent "press for excellence" as a contributor to increased dropout problems. MacMillan, Hendrick, and Watkins (1988) discussed the potential problems encountered by students formerly classified as having borderline mental retardation (IQ 70–85) who became "nonretarded" when the shift in IQ guidelines was enacted in 1973 (Grossman, 1973). These students were decertified in keeping with the push for equal educational opportunity, but they suddenly found themselves being held to graduation standards they were ill equipped to meet. There are students currently enrolled as regular education students who in previous years might have qualified as students with mild disabilities and whose probability of graduating will be dramatically reduced by new policies that require certain courses and minimum-competency-testing requirements for graduation. A recently completed project (MacMillan, Balow, & Widaman, 1991) found that this at-risk, but no longer "disabled," population contributed disproportionate numbers of students to the ranks of dropouts. As teachers participate in establishing graduation requirements, they must be sensitive to the needs of such students. Moreover, teachers must make other policymakers (e.g., school boards, administrators) aware of the existence of this population in the schools and the implications of policies for these students. Policies such as the shift in guidelines affect both students with disabilities and those who are at risk of dropping out. Frequently, such policies are enacted with good intentions, but they have unanticipated effects on segments of the school population.

Suggestions for Administrators

Administrators can generate different dropout estimates for their district that minimize or maximize the dropout problem. They should strive for valid estimates that truly reflect the magnitude of the dropout problem in their district or school.

One lesson to be learned from the various national estimates of the dropout rate is that variations in definition, criteria, and accounting procedures can result in vastly discrepant estimates of the dropout problem. Consider some of the practices encountered in different school districts. One district gives every student withdrawing from school a copy of his or her transcript. That district defines a dropout as a student no longer attending the school for whom no request for a transcript has been received. If a student is given a transcript when he or she withdraws, that student will *not* be counted as a dropout even if he or she does not subsequently enroll in another school. Another district assumes that all students who move out of its boundaries are attending school without confirming that to be the case. Such practices serve to minimize the dropout rate reported by the district and permit the district to report lower dropout rates than are probably accurate. Other practices also distort estimates of the true rate of dropping out. For example, a substantial number of dropouts return to school at a later date. Some districts assign these students new student identification numbers. If such a student subsequently drops out again before graduating, he or she will be counted twice, thereby increasing the dropout rate for the district. Clearcut criteria for establishing whether or not certain cases should be counted as dropouts need to be established. Sometimes state criteria are mandated; if so, it should be clear to the administrator how certain cases are counted. Here the focus is on unusual situations such as students who die, those who are transferred to continuation high schools (alternative schools enrolling students who have been suspended from or do not fit in comprehensive high schools), or those who take a state equivalency examination for the GED.

Administrators have, on occasion, generated figures that serve their own purposes. For example, engaging in practices that minimize the dropout rate may be useful when attempting to portray the district or school as being successful in preventing dropouts. Such figures might be used when reporting to school boards. Conversely, when asking for funds to establish a dropout prevention program, administrators might find it useful to report a high dropout rate. Accounting procedures and criteria that yield high rates might then be employed. Therefore, to interpret dropout rate figures intelligently, it is necessary to understand the definition employed, the criteria used, and the accounting procedures.

Administrators must take steps to remedy those school factors that are related to high dropout rates that are amenable to change.

In the review of research, several school factors were noted as being related to schools with high dropout rates. Among these factors were overcrowding, a high level of feelings of disempowerment among staff, tracking, weak leadership by the principal, and order and discipline problems. Additional factors such as low general achievement and being an inner-city school are status factors, which cannot be changed, or indicative of other child and family features. For the district administrator, changing principals, if weak leadership is the problem, is a possibility. Overcrowding is often an economic problem; yet the administrator ought to be sensitive to it and at least advocate that steps be taken to reduce enrollment at that site. Changes in policy or personnel can be considered when addressing the empowerment of staff and any problems that exist with order and discipline. These factors are amenable to change, and it is the responsibility of administrators at the district and school building level to consider them carefully.

Administrators must analyze prevention programs to ensure that the elements of a particular prevention program are responsive to the student and school factors of greatest concern in that particular district or school.

Dropout prevention programs address presumed causes of the decision to drop out. Some emphasize academic skill building on the assumption that the reason students drop out is that they are doing poorly in academics. These prevention programs might be responsive to students who are struggling academically; however, they are unlikely to address the needs of students whose decision to drop out hinges on pregnancy, economic need, or substance abuse. Other kinds of intervention components will have to be instituted to address these reasons.

Administrators are responsible for deciding which, if any, dropout prevention efforts will be instituted in their districts. They must be aware of the local student constituency and the primary reasons for dropping out of school. In kind, they must examine the variety of prevention programs available to determine the features of these programs and how they might address the most common reasons for dropping out among their students in their districts or schools. It is naive to assume that there is a dropout prevention program that will work equally well in all districts for all dropouts.

Administrators must critically analyze the evaluation data on the effectiveness of the various dropout prevention programs in deciding on which programs to institute in their districts.

Dropout prevention programs are advertised that present few, if any, evaluation data regarding their efficacy. Programs that have not been evaluated should not be adopted; if they are adopted, the district must evaluate them. For those programs that *have* been evaluated, administrators must examine and evaluate the evidence regarding their effectiveness, considering the types of settings in which the evaluation was undertaken (i.e., is there a match between the settings—urban, low achievement?), the level of evaluation performed (i.e., formative or summative), and the overall design and quality of analyses.

Recovery of dropouts who re-enroll in school might well justify the expenditures needed to retrieve those who leave school.

The economics involved in a student's discontinuing his or her schooling are considerable when the number of dropouts becomes great. The loss in income to the district merely in terms of lost average daily attendance (ADA) reimbursement is considerable. A number of dropouts are unaware that they can transfer to other schools within the district, that a continuation school exists, or that assistance is available in the school. The salary of one person assigned to follow up on dropouts would easily be recaptured if this person were able to persuade several students who had dropped out to return to school. This person could operate out of the child welfare and attendance office, which is usually responsive to students who are underage for leaving school. However, when dropouts are over the legal age to leave school, districts show less persistence. Administrators should carefully cost out the economics of recapturing dropouts of all ages.

4. Program Implications

Efforts to reduce the number of dropouts require the establishment of reliable and valid estimates of the magnitude of the problem. Issues include how diplomas versus certificates will be counted and how GED completers will be recorded. Dropout prevention programs must take into account the reasons students leave, which are not necessarily the same as those factors that predict dropping out.

The research literature on school dropouts can be seductive. Although the literature is extensive, we must be careful to understand what we *do* know as opposed to what we have yet to learn. For example, recent policy statements have targeted a goal of reducing dropouts to 10% or less. It might seem logical, then, to estimate the current dropout rate and calculate how much we need to reduce it to achieve the 10% goal. As noted in the "Synthesis of Research" section of this booklet, however, we do not know the precise magnitude of the dropout problem among students with disabilities or, for that matter, those without disabilities. Rather, various agencies make estimates using different cohorts, different criteria, and different methods to account for student attendance, graduation, or dropout rates. Therefore, the first step, estimating the current dropout rate, is not clearly understood. Reducing the dropout rate suggests that we know what causes students to drop out and can design interventions that target these reasons.

Establishing Dropout Rates

It is crucial that program personnel critically evaluate rates reported by the federal agencies. National averages mask considerable variability in dropout rates that exist regionally, for states, for districts, and even for schools within districts. For example, if the graduation rate is estimated nationally to be 75%, it does not follow that 25% of students drop out. As noted earlier, included among the residual count (those who did not graduate on time) are cases of students requiring an additional year to complete high school, those who took state equivalency examinations and the GED, those who entered college early, and a host of other successful students who have the option of continuing into higher education or can state to potential employers that they completed high school.

Kominski (1990) has provided the most compelling arguments for using a standard 1-year period for estimating dropout rates. He reasons that the term *rate* implies the number of occurrences of an event (e.g., dropping out) over a specified period of time. When he evaluated the data from the Bureau of the Census and from the *High School and Beyond* data set, he concluded that approximately 5% of a grade cohort drops out in a given year, with 5% of those remaining dropping out the next year. In other words, the national average of 10th graders dropping out of school is 5%; however, in the 11th grade another 5% of the remaining students can be expected to drop out. For local program administrators, however, using this 5% figure is risky if the districts in which they work are atypical—that is, are serving a student population at greater or lesser risk for dropping out or in a district that may be at risk for higher or lower dropout rates.

The first step, then, in establishing any dropout program, is to establish a local baseline rate for dropping out. Until this rate is established it is impossible to determine whether or not interventions are reducing the rate at which students drop out of school. Since higher rates are expected in inner-city schools than in suburban schools, an individual baseline rate for dropouts provides a local rate against which to compare the impact of any intervention.

Similarly, local baseline rates should probably be established for specific schools. For example, continuation high schools tend to have much higher dropout rates than do traditional high schools, largely because continuation high schools serve students who have had academic or behavioral difficulties at the traditional high schools. Averaging the high school dropout rates across high schools in a district masks variations in rates attributable to student/home characteristics of the student body and yields an estimated rate that may be inappropriate for any single school.

Administrators must also be cautious about evaluating the success of a given school by comparing dropout rates. Too often, people make direct comparisons between schools on the basis of achievement test scores or dropout rates and make inferences about the quality of education being provided based on these data. The notion that the school with the highest achievement test scores or the lowest dropout rates must be providing the best quality of education is fallacious. Usually, the school with the highest achievement test scores and the lowest dropout rates is the school serving students who come from the most affluent homes and have parents whose educational attainments are the highest. Differences in dropout rate are related to the urban-suburban dimension, achievement level of students, socioeconomic status of the student body, and a host of other dimensions along which students and their homes differ.

Baseline dropout rates should also be computed separately for special education students. As noted in the review of research, there is reason to believe that students with mild disabilities (LD and ED, specifically) drop out in greater proportions than do students without disabilities. Also noted was the need for research that examines whether or not the same predictors of dropping out exist for students with disabilities as for students without disabilities. It is important to consider that many students with mild disabilities are mainstreamed for substantial proportions of the school day. As a result, care must be taken in attributing dropping out to failures of special education services. Special education students drop out of school—not out of *special education*. Because they constitute such a small percentage of the total high school enrollment, their numbers do not dramatically impact total school figures. Nevertheless, by calculating special education dropouts separately, it is possible to determine whether or not attrition is comparable across specific disability groups and between special education and general education students.

Establishing Graduation/Completion Criteria

Documents given to students who complete a program of study at the high school level vary. In many states, special education students who do not meet all standard high school requirements for graduation (e.g., do not pass minimum competency tests or do not take prescribed courses) are not granted a high school diploma. Usually these students receive some sort of certificate of completion, which symbolizes that they remained in school for a prescribed period of time and completed a program of study that, while appropriate for them, somehow differed from the standard program of study. Other students take and pass GED examinations or state equivalency examinations and are recognized as *completers*, but are not awarded a standard diploma. Such variances from the standard program of preparation and differences in the type of exiting document can be, although it need not be, troublesome to those estimating dropout rates.

Those who estimate numbers of graduates based on dichotomous outcomes (i.e., either you graduate or you do not) must decide how to categorize students who complete an alternative preparation program. Are they to be counted as graduates or in the residual category? In the past, the reports by states on graduates, which are summarized by the U.S. Department of Education, have defined a graduate as a person who *receives a standard diploma*. In essence, this forces all other completers (e.g., certificate recipients, those passing the GED) to be counted in the residual category (presumably nongraduates). This is misleading if the residual category is somehow interpreted to constitute a dropout population, because a student who completes a program of study to the satisfaction of the school district represents a very different outcome from one who voluntarily leaves school before completing a program of study.

This has been a particular problem in considering special education students because of the trend toward using graduation data as an index of educational quality. If "good" programs graduate high percentages of students, then any student who "counts against" graduation rates is perceived by program administrators as a problem. Take, for example, special education students in a state that uses certificates as an exiting document for any student who does not complete the standard program. These students are counted as nongraduates in the residual category interpreted by some to constitute the failure of the educational system to retain them through graduation. In fact, they are completers of prescribed programs.

One possible solution to this problem is being considered by the Council of Chief State School Officers. The proposal is for school completers to be tabulated under descriptive categories that differentiate those who receive standard diplomas from those who complete high school via alternative routes. Among the types of completers to be counted and differentiated under this proposal are

- Traditional high school diploma recipients.

- Nontraditional high school diploma recipients.

- Other certificate/credential recipients.

- GED credential recipients.

Such a breakdown permits calculating an overall completion rate (i.e., summing all cases across these four categories) and calculating by the type of exiting document received.

Program administrators must recognize that various routes to school completion exist and that different exiting documents are granted. Any accounting system instituted should capture the complexity of the issue, not simply dichotomize students into diploma recipients and another residual category.

Adopting Prevention Programs

Efforts to reduce the number of students dropping out require districts and schools to institute interventions, and district personnel must match program components with reasons why students leave school early. As noted previously, the research base to date emphasizes *predictors* of early school leaving, which are not necessarily the *reasons* students drop out. It is naive to assume that because low achievement is one predictor of school dropout the prevention program must be an academic program designed to remediate achievement problems. Special education services provided to many students with learning disabilities are, in fact, designed to remediate academic problems in small groups; yet the dropout rate of these high school students appears to be as high as, or higher than, that of the general school population.

It is difficult to design effective prevention programs because we are not certain of the reasons why students are leaving school. Moreover, the reasons are frequently multiple (e.g., a young woman is pregnant, low achieving, and poor), and they vary from student to student. In addition, it is unclear whether the so-called "objective" data (e.g., grade point average, standardized achievement test scores) are as useful as the students' perceptions (e.g., "I am a poor student" despite an adequate GPA) in prompting the decision to leave school early. Most of the research has used these objective measures as variables in attempting to predict dropouts because these data are more readily available to researchers and they have, in fact, been predictive.

Successful prevention programs must also be cost efficient. That is, administrators do not want to assign students to expensive prevention programs who are not considering dropping out of school. Instead, the services should be targeted at those students who are, in fact, at risk for dropping out. In this context, some programs do make it possible to predict school dropouts. For example, the Systematic Screening for Behavior Disorders (SSBD) (Walker & Severson, 1990) consists of a three-stage screening program that yields data highly predictive of students likely to drop out of school. Project RIDE (Responding to Individual Differences in Education) is designed to accommodate problem learners in regular classes and to increase school success for at-risk children, thereby reducing the risk of dropout (Beck, R., 1990). Another intervention program, the Accelerated Schools Program (Levin, H., 1987), which was developed at Stanford University, is designed to meet the educational and social needs of at-risk students. It entails involvement by an array of community resources, modification of structure of the school, and an extended-day program to bring at-risk students to grade level. Such programs require training of staff, and all have been field tested and report evaluation data on their success.

Perez-Selles (1989) has described a variety of programs in operation. These programs vary considerably in the age of the target students (e.g., primary grades vs. high school) and the extent to which they involve parents and community volunteers. A total of 41 programs are briefly described as "successful"; these are categorized under the following headings: Academic Support, Case Management, Family Crisis Programs, Alternatives to Suspension, Peer Programs, Programs for Non-English-Speaking Students, Curriculum Enhancers, Counseling, Teacher Training, Health Programs, and Alternative Schools/Programs. Under each of these headings, Perez-Selles has described specific programs, along with addresses and phone numbers for contact persons involved in the programs. Reviews of such descriptors might enable administrators to identify potentially viable programs and permit gathering of information on the viability of programs for specific districts.

Again, program directors will have to examine programs and ascertain the extent to which they address the populations in their particular schools and whether or not program components are responsive to the particular reasons students in their district are leaving school before graduation. Local program directors must critically analyze field test evaluation data in an effort to determine the strength of the evidence for the prevention of school dropouts.

References

Arnold, G. (1985). *A profile of Illinois dropouts.* Springfield: Department of Planning, Research, and Evaluation, Illinois State Board of Education. (ERIC Document Reproduction Service No. ED 262 314)

Barro, S., & Kolstad, A. (1987). *Who drops out of high school? Findings from high school and beyond.* Washington, DC: U.S. Department of Education/OERI.

Beck, R. (1990). *Project R.I.D.E.* Sopris West Inc., P.O. Box 1809, Longmont, CO 80502-1809.

Bernoff, L. (1981). *Early school leavers: High school students who left school before graduating, 1979–80* (Publication No. 404). Los Angeles: Research Branch, Los Angeles Unified School District. (ERIC Document Reproduction Service No. ED 218 385)

Carnegie Corporation. (1989). *Turning points: Preparing American youth for the 21st century.* (Reprint of the Task Force on Education of Young Adolescents). New York: Author.

Catterall, J. S. (1988/1989). School dropouts: Here today, here tomorrow. *UCLA Journal of Education, 3*(1), 27–42.

Edgar, E. (1987). Secondary programs in special education: Are many of them justifiable? *Exceptional Children, 53,* 555–561.

Ekstrom, R. B., Goertz, M. E., Pollack, J. M., & Rock, D. A. (1986). Who drops out of high school and why? Findings from a national study. *Teachers College Record, 87,* 356–373.

Fafard, M. B., & Haubrich, P. A. (1981). Vocational and social adjustment of learning disabled young adults: A followup study. *Learning Disability Quarterly, 4,* 122–130.

Fardig, D. B., Algozzine, R. F., Schwartz, S. E., Hensel, J. W., & Westling, D. L. (1985). Postsecondary vocational adjustment of rural, mildly handicapped students. *Exceptional Children, 52,* 115–122.

Fine, M. (1986). Why urban adolescents drop into and out of public high school. *Teachers College Record, 87,* 393–409.

Frase, M. J. (1989, September). *Dropout rates in the United States: 1988.* (NCES, Analysis Report, 89-609). Washington, DC: U.S. Department of Education, National Center for Education Statistics.

Grossman, H. J. (Ed.). (1973). *Manual on terminology and classification in mental retardation.* Washington, DC: American Association on Mental Deficiency.

Handler, H. (1988/1989). Response. *UCLA Journal of Education, 3*(1), 43–45.

Hasazi, S. B., Gordon, L. R., & Roe, C. A. (1985). Factors associated with the employment status of handicapped youth exiting high school from 1979 to 1983. *Exceptional Children, 51*, 455–469.

Hess, G. A., & Lauber, D. (1985). *Dropouts from the Chicago public schools: An analysis of the classes of 1982, 1983, 1984.* Chicago: Panel on Public School Finances. (ERIC Document Reproduction Service No. ED 258 095)

Hewitt, S. K. N. (1981). *Learning disabilities among secondary in-school students, graduates, and dropouts.* Doctoral dissertation, University of Minnesota, Minneapolis.

Jay, E. D., & Padilla, C. L. (1987, August). *Special education dropouts: The incidence of and reasons for dropping out of special education in California.* Menlo Park, CA: SRI International.

Kominski, R. (1990). Estimating the national high school dropout rate. *Demography, 27*, 303–311.

Levin, E., Zigmond, N., & Birch, J. (1985). A follow-up study of 52 learning disabled students. *Journal of Learning Disabilities, 18*, 2–7.

Levin, H. M. (1987). Accelerated schools for disadvantaged students. *Educational Leadership, 44*(6), 19–21.

Lichtenstein, S. J. (1987). *A study of selected post-school employment patterns of handicapped and nonhandicapped graduates and dropouts.* Doctoral dissertation, University of Illinois at Urbana-Champaign.

MacMillan, D. L., Balow, I. H., & Widaman, K. F. (1991). *A study of minimum competency tests and their impact: Final Report.* Riverside, CA: University of California, Riverside.

MacMillan, D. L., Balow, I. H., Widaman, K. F., Borthwick-Duffy, S., & Hendrick, I. G. (1990). Methodological problems in estimating dropout rates and the implications for studying dropouts from special education. *Exceptionality, 1*, 29–39.

MacMillan, D. L., Hendrick, I. G., & Watkins, A. V. (1988). Impact of Diana, Larry P., and PL 94-142 on minority students. *Exceptional Children, 54*, 426–432.

MacMillan, D. L., Widaman, K. F., Balow, I. H., Borthwick-Duffy, S., Hemsley, R. E., & Hendrick, I. G. (in press). Special education students exiting the educational system. *The Journal of Special Education.*

McDill, E. L., Natriello, G., & Pallas, A. M. (1985). Raising standards and retaining students: The impact of the reform recommendations on potential dropouts. *Review of Educational Research, 55*, 415–433.

McDill, E. L., Natriello, G., & Pallas, A. M. (1986). A population at risk: Consequences of tougher school standards for student dropouts. *American Journal of Education, 94*, 135–181.

New York City Board of Education. (1985). *The 1983–84 dropout rate.* Brooklyn, NY: Author.

Office of Special Education Programs, U.S. Department of Education. (1987a). *Ninth Annual Report to Congress on the Implementation of the Education of the Handicapped Act.* Washington, DC: Author.

Office of Special Education Programs, U.S. Department of Education. (Feb. 1987b). *State education statistics (Wall Chart).* Washington, DC: Author.

Office of Special Education Programs, U.S. Department of Education. (1988). *Tenth Annual Report to Congress on the Implementation of the Education of the Handicapped Act.* Washington, DC: Author.

Office of Special Education Programs, U.S. Department of Education. (1989). *Eleventh Annual Report to Congress on the Implementation of the Education of the Handicapped Act.* Washington, DC: Author.

Office of Special Education Programs, U.S. Department of Education. (1990). *Twelfth Annual Report to Congress on the Implementation of the Education of the Handicapped Act.* Washington, DC: Author.

Peng, S. S., & Takai, R. R. (1983). *High school dropouts: Descriptive information from* High School and Beyond. *National Center for Education Statistics Bulletin.* Washington, DC: National Center for Education Statistics. (ERIC Document Reproduction Service No. ED 236 366)

Perez-Selles, M. E. (1989). *Support services for at-risk youth.* Andover, MA: The Regional Laboratory for Educational Improvement of the Northeast and Islands.

Rumberger, R. W. (1987). High school dropouts: A review of issues and evidence. *Review of Educational Research, 57*(2), 101–121.

Rumberger, R. W., Ghatak, R., Poulos, G., Ritter, P. L., & Dornbusch, S. M. (1990). Family influences on dropout behavior in one California high school. *Sociology of Education, 63,* 283–299.

Walker, H. M., & Severson, H. H. (1990). *Systematic screening for behavior disorders.* Sopris West Inc., P.O. Box 1809, Longmont, CO 80502-1809.

Westat. (October, 1990). *Counting secondary school completers: Threats to the comparability of the OSEP exiting data.* Washington, DC: Office of Special Education Programs, U.S. Department of Education.

Westat. (February, 1991). *OSEP task force for the improvement of data on school exit status: Draft recommendations.* Washington, DC: Office of Special Education Programs, U.S. Department of Education.

Wolman, C., Bruininks, R., & Thurlow, M. (1989). Dropouts and dropout programs: Implications for special education. *Remedial and Special Education, 10,* 6–20, 50.

Zigmond, N., & Thornton, H. (1985). Follow-up of postsecondary age learning disabled graduates and dropouts. *Learning Disabilities Research, 1,* 50–55.

Resources

Bachman, J. G. (1972). Dropouts are losers says who? *Today's Education. NEA Journal, 61*(4), 26–30.

Beacham, H. C. (1980). *Reaching and helping high school dropouts and potential school leavers* (Final Report, Project No. DVE 2-1F11). Tallahassee: Florida A & M University. (ERIC Document Reproduction Service No. ED 236 451)

Beck, L., & Mulia, J. A. (1980). A portrait of a tragedy: Research findings on the dropout. *The High School Journal, 64*(2), 65–72.

Blair, G. E. (1970). *An experiment in educating high school dropouts: An evaluation of the New York Urban League Street Academy Program.* New York: Human Affairs Research Center. (ERIC Document Reproduction Service No. ED 115 705)

Brantner, S. T., & Enderlein, T. E. (1973). Identification of potential vocational high school dropouts. *Journal of Industrial Teacher Education, 11*, 44–52.

Bryan, T., Pearl, R., & Herzog, A. (1989). Learning disabled adolescents' vulnerability to crime: Attitudes, anxieties, experiences. *Learning Disabilities Research, 5*, 51–69.

Bureau of the Census, U.S. Department of Commerce. (1986). *School enrollment—Social and economic characteristics of students: October 1983.* (Current Population Reports, Series P-20, No. 413). Washington, DC: Author.

California Assembly Office of Research. (1985). *Dropping out, losing out: The high cost to California.* Sacramento: Joint Publications Office, State of California.

Cardon, B. W., & French, J. L. (1966). *Employment status and characteristics of high school dropouts of high ability.* University Park: Pennsylvania State University. (ERIC Document Reproduction Service No. ED 010 978)

Carlson, E. (1990, February 27). *National data trends and issues: Description of upcoming DRC study.* Paper presented at the Office of Special Education Conference on the Management of Federal/State Data Systems, Crystal City, VA.

Catterall, J. S. (1986). Dropping out: The cost to society. *Education* (UCLA), *4*, 9–13.

Center for Field Research and School Services. (1973). *An evaluation of high school redirection program.* New York: New York University Center for Field Research and School Services. (ERIC Document Reproduction Service No ED 091 454)

Combs, J., & Cooley, W. W. (1968). Dropouts: In high school and after high school. *American Educational Research Journal, 5,* 343–363.

Cox, J. L., et al. (1985). Study of high school dropouts in Appalachia. Triangle Park, NC: Center for Educational Studies. (ERIC Document Reproduction Services No. ED 264 992)

Doss, D. A. (1984). *Desegregation and dropping out in one school district* (Austin Independent School District). Austin: Texas Office of Research and Evaluation. (ERIC Document Reproduction Service No. ED 247 353)

Fine, M., & Rosenberg, P. (1983). Dropping out of high school: The ideology of school and work. *Journal of Education, 165,* 257–272.

Frazier, D., & Stone, S. (1983). *Barriers to student completion of vocational programs, final report.* Stillwater: Oklahoma State Department of Vocational and Technical Education. (ERIC Document Reproduction Service No. ED 237 686)

Gallington, R. O. (1966). *The fate and probable future of high school dropouts and the identification of potential high school dropouts.* Carbondale: Southern Illinois University (ERIC Document Reproduction Service No. ED 258 095)

Hahn, A. (1987). Reaching out to America's dropouts: What to do? *Phi Delta Kappan, 69,* 256–263.

Hamilton, S. F. (1986). Raising standards and reducing dropout rates. *Teachers College Record, 87,* 411–429.

Hammack, F. M. (1986). Large school systems' dropout reports: An analysis of definitions, procedures and findings. *Teachers College Record, 87,* 324–341.

Hill, C. R. (1979). Capacities, opportunities and educational investments: The case of the high school dropout. *Review of Economics and Statistics, 61,* 9–20.

Hoffman, L. (1990, February 27). *Update on the National CES Dropout Study.* Paper presented at the Office of Special Education Programs Conference on the Management of Federal/State Data Systems. Crystal City, VA.

Hoyt, K. B., & Van Dyke, L. A. (1958). *The drop-out problem in Iowa high schools.* Des Moines: State Department of Education. (ERIC Document Reproduction Service No. ED 002 793)

Jordan-Davis, W. E. (1984). *The cry for help unheard: Dropout interviews.* (Austin Independent School District). Austin: Texas Office of Research and Evaluation. (ERIC Document Reproduction Service No. ED 248 413)

Kaufman, M. J., Kameenui, E. J., Birman, B., & Danielson, L. (1990). Special education and the process of change: Victim or master of educational reform? *Exceptional Children, 57,* 109–115.

Mann, D. (1986). Can we help dropouts: Thinking about the undoable. *Teachers College Record, 87,* 307–323.

McClelland, D. C. (1968). *Achievement motivation training for potential high school dropouts.* (Achievement Motivation Development Project Working Paper No. 4). Cambridge: Harvard University Graduate School of Education. (ERIC Document Reproduction Service No. ED 029 067)

Morrow, G. (1986). Standardizing practice in the analysis of school dropouts. *Teachers College Record, 87,* 342–355.

Natriello, G. (1984). Problems in the evaluation of students and student disengagement from secondary schools. *Journal of Research and Development in Education, 17,* 14–24.

Natriello, G. (1986). School dropouts: Patterns and policies. *Teachers College Record, 87,* 305–306.

Natriello, G., Pallas, A. M., & McDill, E. L. (1986). Taking stock: Renewing our research agenda on the causes and consequences of dropping out. *Teachers College Record, 87,* 430–440.

Office for Dropout Prevention. (1985). Keeping students in school: Dropout data, research, and programs. Raleigh: North Carolina State Department of Public Instruction. (ERIC Document Reproduction Service No. ED 265 430)

Orr, M. T. (1987). *Keeping students in school. A guide to effective dropout prevention programs and services.* San Francisco: Jossey-Bass.

Owings, J., & Stocking, C. (1986). *High school and beyond, a national longitudinal study for the 1980s. Characteristics of high school students who identify themselves as handicapped.* Washington, DC: National Center for Education Statistics. (ERIC Document Reproduction Service No. ED 260 546)

Prestholdt, P. H., & Fisher, J. L. (1983). *Dropping out of high school: An application of the theory of reasoned action.* Paper presented at the annual meeting of the Southeastern Psychological Association, Atlanta. (ERIC Document Reproduction Service No. ED 244 178)

Rumberger, R. W. (1983). Dropping out of school: The influence of race, sex, and family background. *American Educational Research Journal, 20,* 199–220.

Rumberger, R. W. (1986). High school dropouts: A problem for research, policy, and practice. *California Public Schools Forum, 1,* 1–19.

Scales. H. H. (1969). Another look at the drop out problem. *Journal of Educational Research, 62,* 339–343.

Shaw, L. B. (1982). High school completion for young women: Effects of low income and living with a single parent. *Journal of Family Issues, 3,* 147–163.

Steinberg, L., Blinde, P. L., & Chan, K. S. (1984). Droppirg out among language minority youth. *Review of Educational Research, 54,* 113–132.

Stephenson, R. S. (1985). *A study of the longitudinal dropout rate: 1980 eighth-grade cohort followed from June, 1980 through February, 1985.* Miami: Dade County Public Schools.

Stetler, H. G. (1959). *Comparative study of Negro and white dropouts in selected Connecticut high schools.* Hartford: Connecticut Commission on Civil Rights. (ERIC Document Reproduction Service No. ED 020 211)

Stoller, D. S. (1967). *A study of longitudinal patterns of failure among high school drop-outs and poorly performing graduates.* Cambridge: ABT Associates. (ERIC Document Reproduction Service No. ED 012 486)

Titone, J. S. (1982). *Educational strategies for preventing students from dropping out of high school.* Palo Alto, CA: R & E Research Associates, Inc.

Tseng, M. S. (1972). Comparisons of selected familial, personality, and vocational variables of high school students and dropouts. *Journal of Educational Research, 65,* 462–466.

Wehlage, G. G., & Rutter, R. A. (1986). Dropping out: How much do schools contribute to the problem? *Teachers College Record, 87,* 374–392.

CEC Mini-Library
Exceptional Children at Risk

A set of 11 books that provide practical strategies and interventions for children at risk.

- *Programming for Aggressive and Violent Students.* Richard L. Simpson, Brenda Smith Miles, Brenda L. Walker, Christina K. Ormsbee, & Joyce Anderson Downing. No. P350. 1991. 42 pages.

- *Abuse and Neglect of Exceptional Children.* Cynthia L. Warger with Stephanna Tewey & Marjorie Megivern. No. P351. 1991. 44 pages.

- *Special Health Care in the School.* Terry Heintz Caldwell, Barbara Sirvis, Ann Witt Todaro, & Debbie S. Accouloumre. No. P352. 1991. 56 pages.

- *Homeless and in Need of Special Education.* L. Juane Heflin & Kathryn Rudy. No. P353. 1991. 46 pages.

- *Hidden Youth: Dropouts from Special Education.* Donald L. Macmillan. No. P354. 1991. 37 pages.

- *Born Substance Exposed, Educationally Vulnerable.* Lisbeth J. Vincent, Marie Kanne Poulsen, Carol K. Cole, Geneva Woodruff, & Dan R. Griffith. No. P355. 1991. 28 pages.

- *Depression and Suicide: Special Education Students at Risk.* Eleanor C. Guetzloe. No. P356. 1991. 45 pages.

- *Language Minority Students with Disabilities.* Leonard M. Baca & Estella Almanza. No P357. 1991. 56 pages.

- *Alcohol and Other Drugs: Use, Abuse, and Disabilities.* Peter E. Leone. No. P358. 1991. 33 pages.

- *Rural, Exceptional, At Risk.* Doris Helge. No. P359. 1991. 48 pages.

- *Double* 3 5282 00315 5945 *Youth in Special Education.* Lynne ..., ... Scavarda, Ronda Simpson-Brown, & Barbara E. Thalacker. No. P360. 1991. 44 pages.

Save 10% by ordering the entire library, No. P361, 1991. Call for the most current price information, 703/620-3660.

Send orders to:
The Council for Exceptional Children, Dept. K11150
1920 Association Drive, Reston VA 22091-1589